P9-ELQ-655

The

AT

Christmas Tree

ROCKEFELLER CENTER

CARLA TORSILIERI D'AGOSTINO AND BYRON KEITH BYRD

Foreword by Willard Scott

First published in 1997 by Lickle Publishing Inc
590 Madison Avenue, New York, NY 10022

Library of Congress Cataloging-in-Publication Data

D'Agostino, Carla Torsilieri.
    The Christmas Tree at Rockefeller Center/
    by Carla Torsilieri D'Agostino
    and Byron Keith Byrd;
    foreword by Willard Scott.
        p.   cm.
    ISBN 0-9650308-7-3
    1. Christmas trees—New York (State)—New
York. 2. Rockefeller Center I. Byrd, Byron
Keith. II. Title.
    GT4989.D34   1997
    394.2663'09747'1—DC21   97-22055
                              CIP

Director, Editorial, Production, and Design:
Charles Davey
Editor: Stephanie Salomon
Production Editor: Stacey Guttman
Senior Designer: Kayley LeFaiver

Printed in Japan by Toppan Printing Company

Dedication

For Geoffrey—*Byron Keith Byrd*

To my father, Carl Torsilieri,

who started his own landscape contracting firm,

Torsilieri Inc., as a young man; and to

my three little brothers, Guy, Marc, and Dean,

who joined forces with their father

and now run the family business

that has delivered Rockefeller Center's

"gift to the people of New York"

for the past fifteen years.

—*Carla Torsilieri D'Agostino*

1934

*T*he project of building Rockefeller Center—one of the largest construction feats ever undertaken in New York City—began in 1931, right in the middle of the Great Depression. The workmen were so grateful to have jobs and receive paychecks, they decided to put up a Christmas tree. It was far from the size and scope that Rockefeller Center would see during the coming years. But I'll bet there has never been a tree dedicated with more appreciation, love, and gratitude than that Christmas tree back in 1931.

Nineteen thirty-four was an important year for me. That's the year I was born. It was this same year that the second *official* Christmas tree was placed at Rockefeller Center, instilling the annual tradition.

I have had the high honor and pleasure to be a part of the Rockefeller Center Christmas tree story from 1981 to 1995. I was there each season when the special trailer and truck turned the corner at Forty-ninth Street with what appeared to be a sleeping giant tightly tied with rope. Once the rig had stopped in front of 30 Rockefeller Plaza, I would climb up on the flatbed and perch myself in the branches of the tree and do the *Today* show weather. I would interview the workers from the landscaping and crane companies.

To New York City, the Christmas tree at Rockefeller Center has become more than a symbol of the holiday season. No matter what your faith or religious belief, the tree, the Channel Gardens, the ice skating rink, the Radio City Music Hall Christmas Spectacular—complete with Rockettes, Santa, and the Nativity story—plus the windows at Saks, always produce feelings of warmth and love. There is no other Christmas tree in the world like the one in the heart of New York, a city known for its magic.

Enjoy and cherish the memories found in this wonderful book, of the trees and holiday festivities you and your family have enjoyed over the years. It is great to be a part of a continuing tradition—the Christmas tree at Rockefeller Center.

Love
William
Scott

The First Tree

*T*he glittering modern-day spectacle that is the Rockefeller Center Christmas tree stands in sharp contrast to its humble predecessors. The first informal tree was erected in 1931, during the Depression, at the construction site of the British Empire Building and La Maison Française at Fifth Avenue and Fiftieth Streets soon after the demolition of brownstones in the area had been completed. The tree was a twenty-foot balsam festooned with garlands and served as a backdrop for construction workers receiving their pay that Christmas Eve. The very first formal tree was erected in 1933 in front of the recently completed RCA Building. There has been a tree at this historic landmark ever since.

Construction workers line up by the tree on Christmas Eve 1931 to receive their weekly wages.

Harold O. Cook, forester, points to the top of the seventy-foot tree in Podunk, Massachusetts chosen for 1959.

The Search

Two Norway spruces vie to become "The Tree." The one on the left could be it.

Robert and William Loughran hold copies of The Most Beautiful Tree in the World, published in 1956 by Wonder Books. The story is about a family whose tree is selected for Rockefeller Center. The Loughrans' tree, in Hurley, New York, was chosen in 1963.

The search for suitable trees occurs year-round. The search committee, consisting of Rockefeller Center's landscape contractor and head gardener, is in the constant process of seeking the perfect specimen. The "committee" extends out to include business associates, friends, and acquaintances, who eyeball possible contenders and pass along tips and recommendations to the decision-makers. In recent years, a helicopter has been utilized to scour the countryside of the New York metropolitan area in order to view sections of landscape not visible from the road by car. When the leaves are off the deciduous trees, the scouts take to the air in hopes of spotting an evergreen treetop towering above its companions or standing alone in a clearing. With the use of maps laid out in grid patterns, a potential tree can be pinpointed for further examination on the ground.

Rockefeller Center also receives hundreds of unsolicited offers of trees. One donor, from New Canaan, Connecticut, told her neighbors for years that the huge tree next to her house would be perfect for Rockefeller Center. Finally, she put pen to paper and wrote to the Center, describing her tree. Although she never dreamed that her letter would even be answered, her tree became "the tree" for 1975. The following year, another unsolicited letter provided the tree, this time from Montclair, New Jersey. What had started out as a five-foot potted living room Christmas tree ended up in the plaza at 30 Rockefeller Plaza in 1976. When these unsolicited offers are received, it must be determined if the current specifications of height (sixty-five feet minimum) and width (thirty feet minimum) are met. In addition, the tree must be grand and dense and have a perfect "Christmas tree" shape. A photograph of people standing next to the tree serves as a handy way to judge the height of a contender. The final decision is made by executives at Rockefeller Center, who try to have the tree selected by the Fourth of July each year.

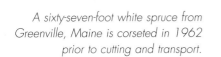

A sixty-seven-foot white spruce from Greenville, Maine is corseted in 1962 prior to cutting and transport.

Corseting

The designated tree is pampered throughout the summer with fertilizing, pruning, and extra watering. In mid-November the landscape contractor's crew begins the "corseting" of the tree. This procedure takes four to seven days and is an integral part of delivering the tree in perfect condition. Three quarters of the bottom branches are individually wrapped in burlap and two-ply twine, drawn up, and strapped to the trunk itself. During the next several days the branches are gradually tightened to reduce the girth to a diameter of twenty feet—the maximum circumference for road clearance on the highways and for access through the toll booths along the tree's travel route. In 1995 the Rockefeller Center landscape contractor devised a hinge system for bending the branches. Larger bottom branches are partially cut and then supported with metal splints and fitted with hinges that enable them to be swept up without snapping. Once the tree is up, the branches are carefully eased down. This procedure has allowed for denser and more massive trees to be taken from the field.

During the corseting of the 1989 tree in Rockland County, New York, Marc Torsilieri, of Torsilieri, Inc., counted the branches as he diligently wrapped them. Subsequently, during an interview with a local New York television news station, he switched roles and asked the interviewer if he had any idea how many branches were on the tree. Taken aback, the broadcaster couldn't even venture a guess and was promptly told that there were 204 limbs on the tree that year.

The 1995 tree from the Mallinckrodt Convent in Mendham, New Jersey on completion of corseting.

23

The 1988 tree proved to be fifty-five years old
after counting its annual rings.

The 1951 Lake Ronkonkoma, New York tree being cut by hand.

Cutting

After the corseting has been completed, the tree is ready for cutting. Press releases have been circulated, and the media arrives in full force. A cabling system is secured to the tree via a ninety-ton crane. When the trunk is cut, the tree is suspended upright, dangling over the newly created stump. As it is swung away, television crews, reporters, and neighbors close in on the remaining trunk to count the annual growth rings that identify the exact age of that year's beauty. In 1951 the tree was cut with a two-man handsaw; since 1953 a chain saw has been used. Once suspended, the tree is tilted up and gingerly placed in its cradle-like trailer. The branches that sweep the ground are then tucked up and protected by a sling that hangs between the tree and the road.

The tree is tilted into position and placed on its trailer.

In 1953 the three-and-a-half foot trunk of the Morristown, New Jersey tree was cut using a chain saw.

Pee Wee hockey players from Saranac Lake, New York pose in front of the 1969 tree as it starts out on its trip to Manhattan (right).

The 1959 tree enters New York state (center).

The 1958 tree, from East Madison, Maine, as it nears its final destination (bottom).

Traveling

The tree is transported over state highways and escorted to an undisclosed rest stop where a police officer assures its safety through the night. In the wee hours of the morning, the truck is back on the road heading toward a bridge to Manhattan (the width of this load does not allow passage through the Hudson River tunnels). The first and only tree to come from outside the United States hailed from Petawawa Forest in Ottawa, Canada in 1966. That 64-foot white spruce covered 550 miles on the way to its destination, the record for traveling distance.

Arrival

Once in Manhattan, the load waits in the still, dark morning along Fifth Avenue. A single strand of yellow safety lights runs along the length of the greenery, resembling the Christmas bulbs that will soon deck its branches. The crew awaits its cue giving the go-ahead to round the corner of Forty-ninth Street and advance to its final destination. With NBC cameras televising the arrival, the tree is safely delivered and the

Passing Saint Patrick's Cathedral on New York's Fifth Avenue, the 1966 tree heads toward Rockefeller Center.

installation process begins. During the day-long untying and setting-up procedures, the crews are visited by cast members of the *Today* show. Bryant Gumbel, Willard Scott, Katie Couric, and Al Roker have all interviewed employees of the landscape firm, the crane company, and Rockefeller Center as they go about the business of raising the tree.

The Radio City Music Hall camels had a nibble on their way past the 1984 tree (top).

At Rockefeller Plaza, 1953 (center).

The end of the journey for the 1987 tree, in front of the RCA Building (bottom).

The Convent Tree

The 1995 Rockefeller Center Christmas tree came from the beautiful grounds of the Mallinckrodt Convent in Mendham, New Jersey. The Sisters of Christian Charity politely but firmly declined when approached in 1984 about parting with their beloved tree. However, when a large tree toppled over on the property during a severe wind storm, they grew concerned about the spruce directly in front of the main entrance to the motherhouse. Planted in 1931 as a sapling, it had grown to seventy-five feet. They worried that it too could come crashing down on the statue of St. Joseph that stood on the sprawling front lawn. They agreed to part with it and to send it off in glory and splendor. The workers came to corset the tree, and the Sisters began to spend more time under its limbs as they realized that it was soon to leave the premises. In past years they had picnicked under its branches and enjoyed the shade it had provided. Now they gathered to celebrate the tree's life by singing songs beneath it and watching the process of preparing it for its big trip to the city. A picture of Sister Lorraine Fatula and her mother was passed around and everyone reminisced over it. The photograph was taken in 1941 when Sister Lorraine first came to the convent. She was only fourteen years old and the tree was only five feet tall! The day of the cutting proved to be bitterly cold and rainy. Inside the convent, however, the Sisters provided hot cider, Christmas music, and warmth for all who came to watch. The crowd gathered round to participate in a tree blessing ceremony:

Sister Lorraine Fatula and her mother in front of the tree in 1941.

Counting the rings of the sixty-four-year old tree.

The motherhouse served as a warm escape from the inclement weather on the day of the cutting.

In May 1997 the Sisters visited "their tree," now a horse obstacle on the grounds of the United States Equestrian Team.

This Tree has given us its shelter and shade in summer's heat,
picnics under its branches,
a nesting place for the birds,
pine cones for baskets and wreaths.
Now, it gives its very life,
We pray that like this tree, we may be generous
in giving ourselves for the sake of others.

The tree was whisked into New York. All 104 nuns went into Manhattan the night of the tree lighting to see it brighten thousands of faces.

The 1960 tree is swung into place with the help of a giant crane.

Workers peer out of the scaffolding surrounding the 1965 tree (inset).

Decorating

Secured with crane cables once again, the tree is suspended at ground level. The star is affixed, and the three-foot stainless steel rod that steadies the tree on its base is drilled into place by carpenters. Rockefeller Center has its own cherished ornament in the four-foot white illuminated plastic star that was crafted by the Center's creative staff during the 1940s. Like a delicate family Christmas keepsake, it is stored in its own special box lined with velvet and pulled out of storage every holiday season. By tradition, this same star has graced the top of the tree for five decades. Other, earlier tree toppers were spiky bursts of colored wood, a huge silver star, and a five-point star outlined in large bulbs.

The project becomes a hard-hat zone for the next phase, which consists of constructing the scaffolding and applying the lights. It takes one to two days to build the scaffolding, with the size of the tree dictating the layers of scaffolding necessary. And just as is done by workers on all buildings, the American flag is anchored to the top of the scaffolding structure. As many as twenty-five electricians begin the arduous task of connecting the bulbs to the tree. The wires, or "streamers," start at the trunk. Each branch is then wrapped out to the end and then back in again. This incredible task can take up to two weeks. The Rockefeller Center tree has been outfitted with amber, green, blue, red, and crystal-colored miniature lights annually since 1969. A brief deviation from this tradition occurred in 1973 when reflecting disks were incorporated to help reduce the number of bulbs used, in keeping with conservation efforts during the energy crisis.

Rockefeller Center's head gardener, David Murbach, presents the star to fellow employees in 1996 (top).

The traditional star is fastened to the top of the 1952 tree (center).

Workers affix ornaments to the upper branches before the tree is raised in 1949 (bottom).

Prior to this tradition of using only colored lights, a variety of seasonal decorations and color schemes had been used. Large multicolored globes were principally used during the 1940s and 50s. Each year the colors would vary. The 1944 tree was hung with sparkling snowflake cutouts accompanied by ten-inch orbs resembling snowballs. The 1950 tree was draped in chains of red and white balls to give the effect of strung cranberries and popcorn. Eleven hundred Christmas lanterns in red, white, yellow, and aqua were used in 1957.

The 1945 and 1946 trees were unique in that the globes were painted fluorescent red, white, green, yellow, orange, and blue. Ultraviolet, or "black," lights made by Kliegl Brothers of New York were then projected onto the fluorescent balls, producing a glowing tree.

Aluminum foil spangles manufactured by Alcoa were introduced for three years in the 1960s. The 1962 tree was done all in gold, with gold spangles. The mid 60s featured large illuminated bells in red, blue, green, and gold accompanied by 6,000 clear lights.

Four-year-old Patty Foster hangs the last snowflake on the 1944 tree.

The year 1936 saw Rockefeller Center erect two matching seventy-foot Norway spruce trees. Each was strung with 2,000 multicolored lights.

The decorated 1945 tree.

Recycling

The big tree was first recycled and returned to the earth in 1971. Ever since, it has been chipped into mulch for use on nature trails in New York City parks and by the Boy Scouts of America at the Winnebago Scout Reservation in Rockaway, New Jersey. Approximately three tons of mulch are generated from the tree. The great trunks have had various afterlives. In recent years the trunk has been used by the Essex Horse Trials at the United States Equestrian Team facility in Gladstone, New Jersey, where it is transformed into jumps and obstacles on the cross-country course. The trunk of the 1987 tree was utilized as the mast of the *H.M.S. Rose* of Bridgeport, Connecticut, and the 1988 tree was planed into planks for use in an addition to the donor's home.

Wood chips fly as the 1971 tree is turned into three tons of mulch (inset).

Chips from the 1972 tree were used as ground cover for a nature trail in New York state.

THIS TREE WILL BE RECYCLED AND RETURNED TO THE EARTH AFTER CHRISTMAS

INFORMATION AVAILABLE AT MAIN DESK · 30 ROCKEFELLER PLAZA

Don Snyder, son of a Rockefeller Center employee, digs a hole for the five-foot specimen that will replace the 1954 tree.

The 1995 tree's trunk is now the Christmas Tree Jump on Stoney Lane at the Essex Horse Trials facility in Gladstone, New Jersey.

The original site of the tree is always restored and usually new specimens are planted there to replace the taken tree. In 1954 a five-foot tree was planted in Belvidere, New Jersey to replace the tree chosen for Rockefeller Center, while the Sisters of Christian Charity in Mendham, New Jersey received a fifteen-foot spruce in 1995. Others choose something different, as Ann Dilger did in 1996. She selected a dogwood and a maple for her property in Armonk, New York.

Reflections

The tree has always reflected the times. It was introduced during an era when hope was needed. In its early years it mirrored the consciousness of society by utilizing nonessential materials and eliminating its lights during wartime. When the war was over, it exploded with color and glowing fluorescence. Currently, during a time of conservation awareness, the tree is recycled, its parts being manufactured into various items. The lights that ornament the tree and the angels in the Channel Gardens are now annual traditions that are familiar and comforting sights.

Known simply as "The Tree," the Christmas tree at Rockefeller Center is the standard against which all other Christmas trees are measured. For the past several decades, over half a million visitors flock daily from all parts of the world to take in the magnificent sight. What is it about this tree that draws throngs of people through crowded streets at such a busy time of year? Why do so many people, and not just New Yorkers, make viewing the tree an annual "must do" tradition? This piece of green nature that is surrounded by a huge mass of glass and concrete fascinates and entices and, for many, sparks a wonder at what is the story behind each year's tree.

"This tree is a gift to the world. I see it as
a message of goodwill and peace on Earth."
—David Murbach, Head Gardener, Rockefeller Center

The Season Begins

officially with the annual lighting

of the Rockefeller Center

Christmas tree. More than one

half million people attend the

event. They huddle together in the

cold and patiently await the

moment when the tree bursts

instantly into a multitude of colors.

Over 26,000 light bulbs on five

miles of wire will mesmerize

the crowds while celebrity hosts,

musical groups, and twinkling

angels provide holiday

entertainment that will long

be remembered.

Broadcasting

The lighting ceremony was televised in 1951 and 1952 on the popular program *Kate Smith's Evening Hour* and seen coast to coast. The following three years, the tree lighting was featured on national television on the *Howdy Doody* show. Through the years, celebrity hosts have included Barbara Walters, Liza Minelli, Arthur Godfrey, and Debbie Reynolds. Monty Hall *(top left)* served as master of ceremonies in 1957, while Johnny Carson *(bottom left)* did the honors in 1964. Media personalities Al Roker and Willard Scott have been known to report the weather seated in or standing beneath the boughs of the tree.

Rodman C. Rockefeller pressed the button that turned the sixty-foot spruce into a bona fide Christmas tree in 1963.

Cameras capture toe-tapping Rockettes, dressed as Santas, performing in the decorated Channel Gardens during the 1989 tree-lighting celebration.

Pageantry

The beautiful 1958 tree stands out amid the bustle of pedestrians, skaters, buses, and cars. The evergreen was a gift from the state of Maine and considered one of the most perfect trees to be erected in Rockefeller Center. It was embellished with 1,000 illuminated red and white globes. Dubbed "the tree that won a beauty contest" by the media, the stunning spruce stood proudly at sixty-four feet high with a branch spread of thirty-six feet.

Ice Festivities

Once the tree has been lit, the festivities are well underway. Most of the action takes place on the ice, with professional skaters entertaining the crowds.

Costumed in vibrant pink and purple, Ken Shelly and Jo Jo Starbuck commanded attention in 1985 *(top left)*.

Donald and Andree Jacoby exhibit the original style that won them the U.S Gold Dance Championships in 1958 and 1959. Their performance in 1961 energized the twenty-ninth annual tree-lighting show *(center left)*.

Immersed in the spotlight, a 1996 ice princess ascends *(bottom left)*.

Skaters from the Center Theater enjoy performing for onlookers in 1947 *(right)*.

Friendly bears assist children on the slippery surface in 1965 (top right).

Twin Canadian skating champions Mary and Margaret Meldrum performed in 1961 (center right).

The 1970 Santa left his sleigh to take a spin on the ice (bottom right).

Ed McMahon and Mitzi Gaynor join G. S. Eyssell, president of Rockefeller Center, for the 1967 festivities (left).

The famous Rockettes and the statue of Prometheus provide the Christmas colors of red and gold in 1983.

First Stanza

Musical entertainment has been present around the tree since its beginning. The 1933 evergreen, considered Rockefeller Center's first official tree, was secured by garland-covered guy wires. Its location is the one used today— on the sidewalk in front of the seventy-story RCA building, which had been completed that May. Christmas music was provided by the Paulist Choristers, the Columbia University Glee Club, the Choir of the Church of the Heavenly Rest, and the Gloria Trumpeters that year. The tree was decorated with 700 blue and white lights, which is quite modest when compared to the 26,000 bulbs that are applied to the tree today.

Then & Now

The Rockefeller Center Choristers delivered their inspiring concert by candlelight in 1939 *(above)*. The vocalists were composed of 190 men and women, all employed by tenant firms in Rockefeller Center. Their director, John R. Jones, led the choir just as passionately as James Hall led the Worship and Praise Choir of Brooklyn in 1996 *(right)*.

Seasonal Sounds

The Shannon Castle Entertainers sang melodic folk songs and Christmas carols from Ireland in 1976 (top left).

Eastern European children taped a 1962 recording of Hungarian song, which was broadcast by Radio Free Europe to the Iron Curtain countries (bottom left).

The colonial era was recalled for the Bicentennial Christmas of 1976 with a fife and drum corps (top right).

Directed by the nationally acclaimed Paul Lavalle, a 1970 brass ensemble donned frock coats, top hats, and mufflers reminiscent of Dickens's day (bottom right).

Ice *Pond*

Skaters inaugurate the new rink on Christmas Day 1936 *(above)*. The rink was originally referred to as the Rockefeller Plaza Outdoor Ice Skating Pond. A later addition to the initial 1931–32 designs for the complex, it has since become a focus of the Center's most sensational season. Over the years, thousands of spectators have been entertained by the razor-sharp blades of Peggy Fleming, Dorothy Hamill, Kristi Yamaguchi, John Curry, and Brian Boitano, among many others. The ice has been graced not only with talented professional skaters but also with the wobbliness and eventual falls of many an enthusiastic novice.

Child's *Play*

Always delighted with the various festivities that surround the tree, children of all ages get lost in their own world as fantasy figures and novelty characters enthrall viewers. Santa and his elves have been joined over the years with friends such as Frosty the Snowman and Snoopy and the Peanuts Gang. Even Mickey and Minnie Mouse took a bow in 1980.

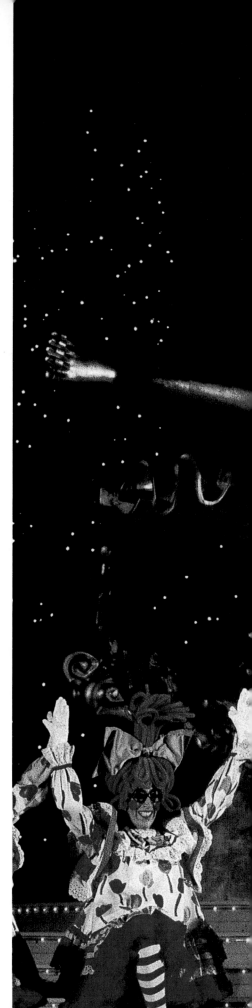

A fantasy figure from 1981 floats on the ice.

The Rockettes, proving they are children at heart, dressed as rag dolls for the 1996 extravaganza.

Santa trades words of wisdom with his elves in 1986 as the 1973 March of Dimes poster child, Paula Pfiefer of Tulsa, Oklahoma, trades autographs with Frank Sinatra, Jr. Sinatra had recently completed an engagement at the Rainbow Room located atop Rockefeller Center on the sixty-fifth floor.

City *Lights*

A surreal mood is captured in 1934 and, sixty years later, in 1994. The earlier tree stood in the center of the lower plaza. Seventy feet tall, it was hung with die-cut figures of Scotty dogs, horses, giraffes, sailboats, and stars.

Patriotic Statement

The year 1942 featured three living Norway spruces. The center tree was
fifty feet tall while its companions were each thirty feet tall. They were live
trees, to be replanted after the holiday season. The center tree was outfitted
in white globes, the left flanking tree in red, and the tree to the right in blue.
It was our second wartime Christmas and only nonessential materials
were used. The trees were not illuminated.

The following year saw an unlit tree as well. The government's request
to conserve fuel by curtailing the use of electricity was honored with the
fifty-five-foot live tree, which was brought in from an estate on Long Island.
Ensigns Jean Graham and Mary Lou Edmondson guard
the 1943 Norway spruce.

American Airlines stewardess Charlotte Macrae assists Rockefeller Center gardener John Buckley in clipping boughs from the 1948 tree. The branches were flown to Los Angeles for pre-Christmas delivery to eighty-one-year-old Samuel Raymond. From newspaper accounts, he recognized the tree as the Norway spruce that grew beside the house in which he was born in Mount Kisco, New York. The evergreen limbs created sentimental household decorations. The spruce ties with the 1996 tree as being the tallest ever on display at Rockefeller Center. Both reached a record-breaking ninety feet.

While the white plastic globes and snowflakes created a nice touch in 1948, they were no match for nature's own decor of a heavy snowfall.

An ethereal snow transforms the 1945 installation into a winter wonderland *(above)*; a ray of sunlight tops the 1949 tree *(left)*. The 1949 tree was sprayed in the field with several hundred gallons of silvery-white paint to simulate a snow-covered look. Five hundred plastic globes in blue, yellow, orange, orchid, and red jump out from this sparkling backdrop during daylight hours, while 7,500 green, yellow, orange, blue, and red bulbs glow at night.

The Channel Gardens

The promenade that runs between the British Empire Building and La Maison Francaise is affectionately known as the Channel Gardens. The name was coined in reference to a comparison of the British and French buildings to their respective countries and the English Channel that flows between them. The pools and plantings with bronze sea nymphs made by René Chambellan in the early 1930s take on an other-worldly look when draped with snow.

Artists Karl Pehme and Valerie Clarebout designed many of the seasonal displays found in the Channel Gardens over the years. English-born Clarebout's sculpted wire angels, which made their debut in 1954, have been featured annually since 1969.

Sculptor Karl Pehme inspects one of his medieval troubadours, colored in antique gold and studded with green, red, and blue synthetic jewels, standing gracefully for the 1966 Christmas display.

Brass and aluminum wire was utilized by Valerie Clarebout to create the fanciful deer that made their way into the 1958 setting.

Little Alycia Lewis greets a new friend in 1961. Nine-foot wire-sculpted snowmen made a merry pathway to the eighty-five-foot tree. The jolly gents carried miniature wire trees dotted with tiny lights and green spangles.

Brilliant Approach

Three hundred red and white tapers formed a processional to the 1953 tree. They were topped with flickering bulbs to simulate actual candlelight and lit the way to the seventy-five-foot, five-ton Norway spruce covered with shimmering icicles.

Stylized starbursts brighten the scene in 1980.

Clusters of candy canes line the path to the 1956 tree. Standing at sixty-four feet, the spruce hailed from New Hampshire. The nine-foot-high peppermint treats enhanced the tree's decorations of red, white, and green.

Different Channels

A forest of twelve-foot-high, ice-blue "Glacite" trees embedded with giant sequins and glass beads makes for an innovative display in 1957.

Ornate figures by Karl Pehme serve up a feast in 1967 beneath glimmering candelabra.

A giant grillwork structure holds 864 multicolored globes and vividly colored Plexiglas inserts in 1960.

The 1963 Christmas tree popped into place with Valerie Clarebout's whimsical wire jack-in-the-boxes.

A peaceful snow provides a frosty blanket for simulated fountains in 1951.

Glittering Gold

The island of Manhattan was transformed into a virtual Land of Oz in 1940 when seventy-two replicas of golden organ pipes, ranging in size from six to nine feet, led to the magnificent eighty-foot tree. More than five decades later, the tree creates a dazzling halo for Prometheus. According to Greek mythology, the Titan Prometheus presented mankind with the gift of fire. The statue weighs eight tons and is cast in bronze and covered in gold leaf. It was sculpted by Paul Manship and installed in January 1934.

Fifties Flair

A fashionable statement was made in the year 1955 as Rockefeller Center

staged the "Swiss Christmas Ice-Travaganza." Featured singers, dancers,

skaters, and a fabulous collection of luxurious winter fashions were flown by

Swissair from Zurich especially for the event. Models, sporting the latest

styles, turned the base of the tree into a veritable runway.

The 1952 tree was dressed with 3,000 feet of Reynolds aluminum garland.

The gleaming evergreen towered at eighty-five feet.

Galaxy of *Stars*

Several major constellations and
the Milky Way are included in a
"ceiling of stars" installation in
1950. More than 500 blue-tinted
lights simulate the stars visible in
New York at 9:00 P.M. on
Christmas Eve. The exact location
for each star was authenticated by
the Hayden Planetarium.

Seasonal rain doubled the beauty of the 1947 and 1990 trees.

*T*win trees were surrounded by snow flurries in 1937. The modern-day version of the tree is surrounded by the flags of the United Nations.

No single Christmas tree in the

world elicits more awe and exudes

1934

1939

1941

1931   1933   1934   1935   1936   1937   1938   1939   1940   1941   1942

50'

Norway Spruce   2 Norway Spruces   Norway Spruce   Norway Spruce
80'   70' each   75'   83'

Babylon, NY   Peter Stuyvesant estate,   NJ estate
                      Allamuchy, NJ

Balsam   Norway Spruce   2 Norway Spruces   70'   Norway Spruce   3 Norway
20'   70'   70' each   88'   Spruces
                                                                                         (living)
                              Private estate,   William Eastwood   50' Center
                              Morristown, NJ   estate,   30' Left
                                                                 Dutchess County, NY   30' Right

1935

1940

1948

1950

1943   1944   1945   1946   1947   1948   1949   1950   1951   1952   1953

Norway Spruce (living) 55'

Norway Spruce 55'

Norway Spruce 65'

Norway Spruce 75' Yaphank, NY

Norway Spruce 82' Lake Ronkonkoma, NY

Norway Spruce 75' William P. Jenks, Morristown, NJ

Norway Spruce (living) 65'

Estate on Long Island, NY

Norway Spruce 75'

Norway Spruce 90' Carl Tucker, Mt. Kisco, NY

Norway Spruce 85' Hollingsworth Wood estate, Mt. Kisco, NY

Norway Spruce 85' Peter Stuyvesant estate, Allamuchy, NJ

1943

1949

1952

1954

1959

1961

1954	1955	1956	1957	1958	1959	1960	1961	1962	1963	1964

Norway Spruce
65'
Belvidere, NJ

White Spruce
65'
Maurice Plante,
Island Pond, VT

Norway Spruce
70'
Harold O. Cook,
Podunk, MA

Norway Spruce
75'
Mr. and Mrs. M.A.
Gilmartin, Jr.,
Smithtown, NY

Norway Spruce
60'
Dr. and Mrs. Elbert J.
Loughran,
Hurley, NY

Norway
Spruce
65'
Belvidere,
NJ

White Spruce
64'
Charles W.
Elliott,
Whitefield, NH

White Spruce
64'
East Madison,
ME

Norway Spruce
65'
Harford, PA

White Spruce
67'
Scott Paper Co.,
Greenville Junction,
ME

Norway
Spruce
60'
Mr. and M
Vito D'Auri
Lake Carme
NY

1958

1960

1967

1971

1965   1966   1967   1968   1969   1970   1971   1972   1973   1974   1975

Norway
Spruce
60'

Mr. and Mrs.
Charles Fagg,
Darien, CT

Balsam
65'

Coventry, VT

Balsam
70'

Saranac Lake, NY

Balsam
65'

Robert Bragg farm,
East Montpelier, VT

Norway Spruce
65'

Tenafly, NJ

Balsam
55'

New
Canaan,
CT

White Spruce
64'

Petawawa Forest,
Canada

White Spruce
55'

Holland, VT

White Spruce
60'

Coventry, VT

Norway Spruce
65'

Old Bridge, NJ

Norway Spruce
63'

Lehighton, PA

1962

1969

1972

109

1978

1983

1986

1976	1977	1978	1979	1980	1981	1982	1983	1984	1985	1986

White Spruce
65'
Dixfield, ME

Norway Spruce
65'
Spring Valley, NY

White Spruce
60'
Danville, VT

Norway Spruce
75'
Mr. and Mrs.
Allan Heinsohn,
Valley Cottage, NY

Norway Spruce
78'
Richard and
Diane Dohl,
Harveyville, PA

Norway
Spruce
68'
Montclair,
NJ

Norway Spruce
75'
Immaculate
Conception
Seminary,
Mahwah, NJ

Norway Spruce
65'
Charles Mapes,
Suffern, NY

Norway Spruce
70'
Immaculate
Conception
Seminary,
Mahwah, NJ

Norway Spruce
75'
Far Hills, NJ

Norway
Spruce
68'
Mary and
Vinnie
Froeling,
Nanuet,
NY

1979

1985

1989

1990

1987   1988   1989   1990   1991   1992   1993   1994   1995   1996   1997

Norway
Spruce
75'

Charles
Mapes,
uffern, NY

Norway Spruce
70'

John Myers,
Suffern, NY

Norway Spruce
65'

Charles Mapes,
Suffern, NY

Norway Spruce
85'

Raymond Cronin,
Pearl River, NY

Norway Spruce
75'

Mallinckrodt
Convent,
Mencham, NJ

Norway Spruce
75'

Rich and Lynn
Luster, Raritan
Township, NJ

Norway Spruce
75'

Shirley Cenci,
West Norwalk, CT

Norway Spruce
65'

Andrew Kupusinkis,
Stony Point, NY

Norway Spruce
85'

Maria and Allan
Eglar,
Ridgefield, CT

Norway Spruce
90'

Ann Dilger,
Armonk, NY

1986

1990

1996

111

Acknowledgments

We wish to thank the following for their support in the creation of this book:

Wanda M. Akin
Sally Bodge
David Brenner
Jeanne Browne
Stefani Michelle Byrd
Devon Cass
Andrea D'Angelo
Charles Davey
Michael Davis
Trent Dickey
Gail Donovan
Stacey Guttman
Carolyn Hannon
Geoffrey Hassman
Jeannette Hektoen
Donald E. Hillner

Karen B. Kane
Nora Keane
Patty Kellert
Herbie and Marcia Klein
Monti Kyle
Sven Larsen
Kayley LeFaiver
William C. Lickle
Lenore Lucey
Jill Lynne
Sandra Manley
Jane and Michael Maas
Andrea Monfried
David Murbach
Michael and Shirley Neal
Michael Pegan
Kenneth A. Perko, Jr.
Susan Price
RCPI Trust

Jim Reed
Diana Rochester
Rockefeller Group, Inc.
Gwen A. Rowden
Elizabeth Ryan
Stephanie Salomon
Andrea Sherman
Elizabeth Slater
Dori Slocum
Brian C. Smith
Barbara Stephenson
Ken Striker
Vince Silvestri
Tishman Speyer Properties
Carl, Lois, Guy, Marc, and Dean Torsilieri
Sister Marion Utz
Robert Van Glahn
Laurie Wynn
    and Jim, Jacie, and Bart.

Photo Credits

We gratefully acknowledge the cooperation of RCPI Trust, Tishman Speyer Properties, Rockefeller Group, Inc., and Rockefeller Management Corporation for the use of its archival photography collection. Every attempt has been made to identify individual photographs for proper credit.

Richard H. Althoff: back jacket, 77
Thomas Andrews: 29 (top left, third from top)
Bart Barlow: front jacket, 1–11, 15, 46 (bottom), 55, 63, 95, 97, 99, 110 (bottom right), 111 (top left, bottom left and right)
Caroline Hood Collection: 86
Cosmo-Sileo: 32 (top), 47, 69, 73, 107 (bottom center)

Carla Torsilieri D'Agostino: 31 (top)
Diana De Rosa: 34 (bottom)
Jackie Freundlich: 29 (bottom)
Walter J. Goetze: 106 (top right)
Impact Photos: 21 (bottom), 27, 40 (bottom), 41, 44–45, 46 (center), 49 (top and bottom), 76 (bottom), 78, 108 (top right and center, bottom right), 109 (top right, bottom left)
International News Photo: 84–85
Wendell MacRae: 32 (center), 66, 106 (top center, bottom left and right)
R. Maiman: 111 (top right, bottom center)
New York State Thruway Authority: 26 (center)
Michael J. Pappas: 29 (second from top)
Michael N. Paras: 42–43, 110 (top center and right)

Bo Parker: 59, 74, 100, 105
Edward Ratcliffe: 25 (bottom left), 31 (center), 34 (top), 40 (top), 68, 71, 80–81, 82 (top), 93, 107 (top left, bottom right), 108 (top left, bottom left)
Robert Reichert: 57 (top), 101
Bob Sacha: 50–51
Saranac Lake Chamber of Commerce: 26 (top)
Sister Lorraine Fatula Collection: 29 (top left)
Guy Torsilieri: 21 (top), 23, 25 (top, center, and bottom right), 28 (bottom)
Wagner International Photos: 33 (right), 56 (top), 57 (bottom), 65, 109 (bottom center)
Wide World Photos: 12–13